The Kids' Guide to
WRITING FICTION

Laurisa White Reyes

Skyrocket Press
28020 Newbird Drive
Santa Clarita, CA 91350
www.skyrocketpress.com

ISBN: 978-1530511945

Cover & interior design by Laurisa White Reyes

TABLE OF CONTENTS

INTRODUCTION:
TO THE STUDENTS

So, you want to write a story. Perhaps you have an idea in mind, but you're not quite sure where to start. Maybe your teacher gave you an assignment, but you just don't think you have it in you to be a writer.

The truth is, anyone can write a story. Have you ever told your parents about something that happened to you at school or at the park? Or raved to your best friend about a movie you watched? If you have, then you are a storyteller.

A storyteller is someone who relates events in a logical order to someone else. For example, if you were to tell someone about your favorite book, chances are you would begin at the beginning. You would share a little information about the characters in the story, go through the major events in the plot, and then conclude with the story's climax.

Every book, every movie, every television show is a story. The author or screenwriter is a storyteller. Think about the last book you read or movie you saw. What story did it tell? On a piece of paper, write a brief summary of the story. Three four sentences should do.

Now think about the story *you* want to write. Imagine it as though it were a movie. Do you know what the opening scene would be? How will it end? Who will be the hero of your story?

Writing a story is a little like building a house. You can't build it all at once. It must be built one brick at a time. The lessons in this workbook are like the bricks you would need to build a house. Each one plays an important role in constructing your story. Read each lesson, and then complete the accompanying worksheets. I recommend you read this book while also reading a novel or short story, and consider how that book puts what you are learning to use. The best way to learn how to write well is to read often. As you progress through your assignments, use the blank lined pages at the back of the book to take notes, brainstorm, and write your story.

You should have at your disposal several writers' tools, including a dictionary, thesaurus, and a book or two on grammar and punctuation. For the latter, I recommend *Eats, Shoots & Leaves* by Lynne Truss. It is very funny and easy to read. Many writers consider Strunk & White's *The Elements of Style* the grammar Bible, though any age-appropriate book on the subject will do.

By the time you reach the end of this workbook, you should have what is called a ***rough draft***. A rough draft is not the finished story. It still has rough edges, spots that need smoothing out, and sections that will need to be rewritten later. The conclusion of this book, "Polishing Your Story," will explain what to do once you have a rough draft.

In the meantime, enjoy the journey that awaits you. You just might discover that writing a great story is even more exciting than telling one.

LESSON #1
CHARACTERIZATION

·◆•◆··◆•◆··◆•◆··◆•◆··◆•◆··◆•◆··◆•◆··◆•◆··◆•◆··◆•◆··◆•◆··◆•◆·

"I *just saw this amazing movie! You've got to see it!"*

Have you ever said these words or something like them before? Maybe it wasn't a movie you raved about, but a book or a television show. Chances are the response you received was a question:

"What's it about?"

"Well," you may have replied, *"It's about this boy (or girl)..."*

Every story begins with one thing in common: *a hero (or heroine)* who somehow captures our imagination and makes us want to root for him all the way to very last second. The hero, or **protagonist**, is the main character of the story, the person we care most about and to whom most events in the story happen.

There may be other characters as well, including a villain (the *antagonist*), friends and family members, and various supporting characters. Like threads woven together in a tapestry, these characters help form a complex and varied texture to a story. Without characters... well, there would be no story.

Like real people, characters have certain characteristics, or traits, that make them unique and memorable. Unlike real people, however, the author gets to pick and choose which traits the characters will have. You create them from your own imagination while drawing on real-life examples for inspiration.

We will discuss four sets of traits that your characters should have: Physical Traits, Psychological Traits, Personality Traits, and Backstory. By imbuing your characters with realistic traits, they will begin to seem lifelike to you and will be easier to bring to life on the page.

PHYSICAL TRAITS

When you meet someone for the very first time, what is the first thing you notice? His eyes? His hair? The way he smiles? Your first impression is usually based on that person's physical appearance. Likewise, a physical description of the protagonist can be found near the beginning of most stories. The description may be brief, just a word or two, or fill half a page. But by the time we, as readers, are invested in the story we have a pretty good idea what the hero looks like.

Physical qualities help us to distinguish one character from another and allow us to form pictures of them in our minds.

Appearance

The most obvious physical traits include gender (male or female), age, ethnicity (race), hair color or style, and eye color. However, appearance should go beyond the obvious. You should consider other details as well, such as body size (height, weight, build), and immediately visible features such as freckles, birthmarks, glasses, scars, tattoos, etc. For example, a female character with flowing blonde hair, a milky complexion, and a tall, slender torso is going to look entirely different than a female with clipped black hair, bulging muscles and a large tattoo on her bicep. The reader will also make automatic judgments about each character based solely on their appearances.

Clothing

You may have heard the saying *clothes make the man*. You can tell a lot about a person by the way he dresses. If you were to see a man wearing a dark suit and tie and carrying a briefcase, you might come to some obvious conclusions about him. He could be a businessman, a lawyer, or a professor. You might assume right off that he is intelligent and educated. But what if this same guy is wearing snakeskin cowboy boots or a pair of worn out Reeboks? Has your perception of him changed? What if he isn't wearing a suit at all, but a pair of denim overalls with a red hanky in the back pocket?

Clothes also reflect the time period in which the character lives. Someone from the Middle Ages, for example, would never be found wearing Levis, nor would a contemporary boy be caught dead in knickerbockers – unless the story was about time travel.

Speech Patterns

Another distinguishing factor can be the way a person talks. This might include accents from various parts of the country or the world, speech impediments like a lisp or stuttering, or even their grammar. You would have a far different view of someone if he greeted you with "Howdy" as opposed to "How do you do." We will discuss speech patterns further in the chapter on dialogue.

Physical Disabilities

Disabilities can be effective in distinguishing your characters from one another, though I would caution you to use them sparingly. The father in the classic novel *The Secret Garden* had a hump on his back. Long John Silver in *Treasure Island* had a wooden peg leg. Kira in Lois Lowry's *Gathering Blue* has a twisted leg and walks with a limp.

The following excerpts are good examples of physical descriptions. The first is from *Rowan of Rin* by Emily Rodda. The second is from *Leven Thumps and the Gateway to Foo* by Obert Skye:

Example #1:

"Sheba scowled as she hunched her shoulders and stared at Rowan. In the firelight her eyes looked red. Her forehead was bound with a purple rag, and her hair hung like thin gray tails around her face. She smelled of ash and dust, old cloth and bitter herbs...She was prodding the cheeses with her bony fingers, sniffing them one by one..." (18)

In this example, we know that Sheba is an old, crotchety woman by her physical appearance. She is hunched over, her hair is long and gray, and she smells of ash, dust, old cloth and bitter herbs. She has bony fingers. The author does not say, "Sheba is old," but we come to that conclusion by the image we form of her in our mind.

Example #2:

"He was fourteen now and so tall that his feet hung off the end of his small bed by a good six inches. His long dark hair was the color of rich mud and on the right side of his head there was a streak of brilliant white hair...He had tried to color the streak, but no matter what he did it remained bright white. Beyond that, he had clear brown eyes, a straight nose, ears that protruded slightly more than most people's, and a large mouth that made him look a bit like a boy who had not completely grown into himself yet, which is what he was." (24)

From this description Leven seems to be a typical teenage boy who is a bit self-conscious about the not-so-typical parts of himself. The fact that he has a streak of white in his hair suggests that there is more to him than meets the eye.

PSYCHOLOGICAL TRAITS

While a physical trait is something you can see or hear, such as hair color or a southern accent, psychological traits are internal, or inside the character where no one else can see them. Psychological traits are characteristics of the mind that make your character unique and can affect the way she thinks, acts and feels throughout the course of your story. For our purposes, we will divide psychological traits into three basic categories: *phobias, weaknesses, and secret problems.*

Phobias

Ask anyone what they fear the most, and it is almost certain you will get an answer. The answers will vary, but everyone is afraid of *something*. Some people are afraid of the dark. Others hate spiders. Still others are terrified of public speaking, of heights, or of dying. Indiana Jones, the hero in the film *Raiders of the Lost Ark*, is afraid of snakes. In one of the early scenes of that film, he finds a boa constrictor in the seat of his getaway plane. He has just faced tarantulas, collapsing caves, angry natives, and villains with guns, but when he meets the snake he comes unglued. His reaction is funny and it makes him seem *real*. He is not this superman-like hero that has no weakness, no chance at losing. We can relate to him, we like him, and because of that we root for him.

Weaknesses

Every character needs a weakness. Otherwise there is no risk of failure. It is that risk that makes a story exciting to read, and the hero's beating the odds that makes us cheer for him in the end. Even Superman has a weakness: Kryptonite, an alien substance that strips him of his powers and makes him like every other human on earth. It is what his archenemy, Lex Luthor, uses against him. Weaknesses can appear in the form of mental disabilities, such as autism (*Al Capone Does My Shirts* by Gennifer Gholdenko), or a terminal illness, like cancer (*Kira-Kira*, by Cynthia Kadohato). Weaknesses can also be funny. Ella from *Ella Enchanted* by Gail Carson Levine was cursed as a child to be obedient. Her weakness is that she must do whatever anyone tells her, often with hysterical results. A weakness could also be an obsession, age, gender, social status, religion, and on and on. Be creative!

Secret Problems

Sometimes the weakness isn't a fear or illness at all, but a problem that torments the protagonist to some degree or another, and may even become her driving motivation in the story. Like fears and weaknesses, most people also have secret problems: discord in marriages or between friends, embarrassing or incriminating events in their past, or a current situation they would like to keep private. Unlike fears and weaknesses, however, these problems do not exist solely inside your character's mind. They are created by her surroundings or relationships. For example, in the Newbery Award winning novel *Walk Two Moons* by Sharon Creech, Sal struggles to come to terms with her mother leaving her. Her feelings of abandonment are the driving force behind the whole plot.

PERSONALITY TRAITS

Aside from how a person looks on the outside, the other most distinguishing feature that makes an individual unique is his personality, or how he behaves in public. Think about someone you know fairly well in real life and consider how that person acts towards others. Is she shy or outspoken? Gentle-natured or aggressive? Controlling or passive? Patient or quick-tempered? Tactless or cautious with her words?

Ella in *Ella Enchanted* is as stubborn as they come and uses her curse of being obedient to get back at those who mistreat her. In the book *Anne of Green* Gables, Anne Shirley is talkative and dreamy, but also has a very hot temper, which often gets her into trouble. The Prince in Sid Fleischman's *The Whipping Boy* is a selfish and spoiled brat.

An easy way to discover your character's personality is to pattern him after someone you know. Eventually, as your story develops, your character will develop his own traits as well, but for the time being draw traits from examples in real life.

BACKSTORY

A character's backstory is a completely different sort of thing than those traits a character is given. It contains details about who he is, where he came from, why he is the way he is, and who are the key players in his life. These elements add depth and realism to the character. There are three basic areas of backstory that should be developed for any character: history, social dynamics, and talents.

History

First, you must know the character's history. Some authors begin with when and where he was born and under what circumstances. Oliver Twist began his life in an orphanage, as did Anne Shirley of *Anne of Green Gables*. They are both orphans whose parents died when they were very young, and were raised in orphanages. Orphans are very popular in fiction because they are the underdog and everyone loves to root for the underdog. (Think Harry Potter, the Baudelaires in *A Series of Unfortunate Events*, and even Mark Twain's *Tom Sawyer*.) That doesn't mean you have to make your protagonist an orphan. But you should have some idea of his past.

Social Dynamics

Second, you as the author must know your character's current situation. Where does he live now and with whom? Does he live with his parents? An aunt? In a boarding school? On the street? Does he go to school? Have a job? Who is his family? Who are his friends? Who else does he come in contact with during the story?

In Kate DiCamillo's book *The Tiger Rising*, the protagonist, Rob, lives in a motel called The Kentucky Star with his father. His mother is dead. During the course of the novel he interacts with several other characters including a prissy girl named Sistine, some bullies named Norton and Billy, and the hotel owner who pays him to feed the caged tiger he keeps out back. We know Rob takes a bus to school and that he likes to go walking in the forest behind the hotel. Social dynamics are the places and people with whom your character interacts.

Talents/Hobbies

The final details of your character's background are his talents. These are the things he is good at, or that interest him in some way. Peter Parker (aka. Spiderman) is a protégé of science, a boy genius. He also has the ability to shoot spider webs from his wrists and climb up the sides of buildings. Maniac Magee, from Jerry Spinelli's novel of the same name, loves to run and is a great problem solver. Harry Potter uses magic. Violet in *A Series of Unfortunate Events* is good at building useful contraptions out of spare parts. Your character might be really good with horses, have superpowers, or is an expert in the field of Egyptian Hieroglyphics. The choice is up to you.

SUMMARY

For readers to relate to the characters in your story, the characters need to be given traits that make them seem like real people. This is called *characterization* and can be divided into three groups: Physical Traits, Psychological Traits, Personality Traits, and Backstory.

Complete the following CHARACTER SKETCH to help develop the characters in your story.

CHARACTER SKETCH

NAME: _____

AGE: _____

GENDER: M F Other _____

ROLE: _____

PHYSICAL TRAITS:
Ethnicity: _____
Eye Color: _____
Build: _____
Hair Style/Color: _____
Glasses/Braces: _____
Skin Tone: _____
Freckles/Birthmarks: _____
Disability: _____
Dress Style: _____
Speech Patterns: _____
Mannerisms: _____ _____

PSYCHOLOGICAL TRAITS:
Phobias: _____
Weaknesses: _____
Secret Problem: _____
Talents: _____

PERSONALITY TRAITS: (Circle all that apply. Add
others as desired.)

    Shy   Pessimistic   Stubborn
               Talkative   Patient

Timid   Short-tempered   Lazy
       Optimistic   Kind
Insecure   Impatient   Tactless
       Organized   Cheerful
Depressed   Cynical   Humorous
       Assertive   Faithful
Morose   Sullen   Gentle
   Confident   Humble

BACKSTORY

Describe your character's history:

_____
_____
_____
_____
_____

Describe his/her social dynamics:

_____
_____
_____
_____
_____

Describe his/her talents and/or hobbies:

_____
_____
_____
_____
_____

LESSON #2
SETTING

•◦•◦•◦••◦•◦••◦•◦••◦•◦••◦•◦••◦•◦••◦•◦••◦•◦••◦•◦••◦•◦•

Once you have your characters worked out, you will need to decide where your story will take place and when. This is called the *setting*.

The setting of a story includes both the location where and time period during which it takes place. The setting might change from scene to scene, or it can remain the same throughout the entire story.

For example, the novel *The Thief Lord* by Cornelia Funke takes place in Venice, Italy. The individual scenes are set in an abandoned movie theater, several homes, an island, etc. The time period in which this story takes place is modern day and follows the characters over the course of several weeks.

In contrast, the short story "An Occurrence on Owl Creek Bridge" by Ambrose Bierce is set during the American Civil War. The entire story takes place on and around a bridge and actually spans only a few moments of time.

Knowing when and where your story takes place is very important and should be decided before you begin writing your first draft.

LOCATION

All stories must take place somewhere, whether in a log cabin in the mountains of Colorado, or a space station in Earth's orbit, or on a ship sailing across the ocean. The location of your story can be anywhere you choose: any country, state or city; any planet or uncharted desert island; any make-believe society your mind can create. No matter where your story takes place, however, you need to be familiar enough with that location to accurately describe it for your readers so that they can picture it in their minds as if they were actually there.

If you set your story on the island of Hawaii, for example, but then describe it as a flat, dry desert, your story will lose credibility. Your readers will not believe you enough to enjoy the story. Even if your story takes place in a land you create, such as Middle Earth in the *Lord of the Rings* trilogy by J.R.R. Tolkien, you should be able to describe it in enough detail so that it sounds real.

Below are two location descriptions. The first, from *Leven Thumps and the Gateway to Foo* by Obert Skye, describes a mobile home park in Oklahoma. The second, a description of a cottage on an imaginary island, is from my own novel, *The Rock of Ivanore*.

"The Rolling Green Deluxe Mobile Home Park was situated on fifty-five acres of Burnt Culvert's finest burnt soil. The town, once named Tin Culvert, had rebuilt itself following a devastating fire that had burned most of It down a few years earlier...Now it housed over one hundred and twenty mobile homes... As soon as the park opened people began to move in and either upgrade or downgrade the area. Some residents planted trees. Some put in lawns. A few built sheds or outbuildings. Some paved tiny slabs of concrete so as to have somewhere to put a picnic table and a barbecue. Others added awnings and outdoor carpeting. Some, of course, did nothing." (14)

Example #2:

"Quendel was not unlike all the other villages east of the Jeweled Mountains, with its clusters of humble cottages and shops connected by narrow cobbled roads. Marcus...never tired of the fragrance of warm bread drifting out of the baker's door, or the nutty scent of freshly ground wheat from the grain mill. Also, the constant clamor of wagons bumping along the road and the bleating and braying of the animals that pulled them were a welcome contrast to the pervasive silence of Zyll's isolated dwelling." (10)

Notice that both locations are described in just enough detail to allow the reader to visualize them in their minds. The mobile home park could be one of any number of similar locations that exist in real life. The cottage in the village of

Quendel does not exist at all, but the way it is described, it seems as though it does.

TIME PERIOD

The other aspect of setting involves the *when* of a story. Will your story take place during medieval England, as in *Crispin* by Avi? Or will it take place in some futuristic society hundreds of years from now, like *Ender's Game* by Orson Scott Card?

The Past

Stories set in the past have many thousands of years from which to choose. Jean M. Auel's adult novel *The Mammoth Hunters* is set in prehistoric times. *Esperanza Rising* by Pam Munoz Ryan is set in California during the Great Depression of the 1930's. A story set in the past could take place as little as five or ten years ago. Often the plot takes place against the backdrop of an actual historical event or person. Familiarity with those events or people is vital. It simply wouldn't do to have your protagonist carry a gun in the year 950 A.D. (unless your story is about time travel) because guns had not yet been invented. Take the time to research the time period in which you want to set your story. Go to the library and check out books or browse related websites. Learn about the key events and figures from that period. Learn how they dressed, how they talked, traveled, prepared food, conducted war, etc. Adding this sort of period-specific information will give your story credibility.

The Present

Many stories are set in present day. That means the characters and events could realistically exist today. There is no need to create "new" technology or to be accurate in describing things as they were in the past. However, if the story takes place today, it is important that the characters dress, act, and speak like real people. No need to write an abundance of slang or mention music, TV shows, etc. that pertain to today's generation to make your story current, but if you do, be aware that five or ten years from now those things will be outdated and so will your story.

The Future

Stories set in the future usually fall into the category of Science Fiction. Authors of Science Fiction are free to represent the future any way they choose. The earth might be overrun with an alien species that enslaves humans, or humans might have evolved to a point where they communicate without speech. A futuristic story might take place on earth, on a distant planet, a parallel dimension, or in an imaginary society. But even though stories set in the future allow the authors to create their own reality, this reality must still be convincing to the reader. If humans on your future earth live in a post-nuclear society, will they have more technology than their forerunners or less? Will they be forced to live in caves and hunt like prehistoric humans? If your futuristic society is technologically advanced, what machines and weapons will they use? What new technology do they use in the fields of medicine, education, agriculture, etc?

SCIENCE FICTION & FANTASY

In case you are wondering what the difference is between science fiction and fantasy, here is a brief explanation. SF is usually set in the future and uses advanced technology: spaceships, laser weapons, anti-gravity boots, etc. Fantasy can be set in the future, but it can also be set in the past or present. Events that take place in fantasy are usually magical or mystical in nature. *The Lord of the Rings* takes place in the far past, long before man became the dominant species of earth, while the book *Midnight Blue* by Pauline Fisk is set in present day and the protagonist rides on a magical balloon to a parallel dimension.

SUMMARY

A book's setting involves the location and time period in which the story takes place. A story can occur anywhere, real or imaginary, and can occur in the past, present or future. The author's task is to make the setting real for the reader through accurate and convincing description.

Complete the following SETTING WORKSHEET to help you visualize the setting of your story.

SETTING WORKSHEET

To help you determine the setting of your story, answer the following questions:

1. Will your story take place in the past, present or future?

_____

2. If your story takes place in the past, what time period are you considering? (For example: the Dark Ages, America's Old West, The Great Depression)

_____

_____

3. What events or people are pivotal to that era?

_____

_____

_____

_____

4. List details that you know about that era, such as clothing styles, modes of transportation, types of housing, etc.

_____

_____

_____

_____

5. Will your story take place in a real or imaginary location?

_____

6. In what country, state or city will it take place?

_____

7. If set in an imaginary location, what is its name?

_____

8. Will your story involve magic, mysticism, or advanced scientific inventions? If so, describe how these elements are connected to your setting:

_____
_____
_____

9. Where does your story begin? (In a house, school room, a field, etc.) Describe this location:

_____
_____
_____

10. List three (3) details about your setting that you plan to research:

A. _____
B. _____
C. _____

11. Using your local library or an online search engine, locate 2 – 3 sources about the details listed above. List one new piece of information about each detail you can use in your story:

1. _____
2. _____
3. _____

LESSON #3
PLOT

•◆•◆•◆•◆•◆•◆•◆•◆•◆•◆•◆•◆•◆•◆•◆•◆•◆•◆•

Just like a story isn't a story without characters, a story is not a story without a *plot*. A simple definition of plot is all the stuff that happens in a story. It is the beginning, middle, and end of a story, but plot is a little more complicated than that. There are certain elements that must be present to make a plot work. The first element is *action*. Your characters must *do* something. They need to move around and talk. However, action alone does not make a story, as the following example shows:

> Susie woke up Tuesday morning. She yawned, stretched, and made her way to the bathroom. Her feet felt cold against the tile floor and she rubbed them against her legs to warm them. She turned on the shower and waved her hand through the water. Then she undressed and stepped in. When her shower was finished she got dressed, ate a bowl of oatmeal for breakfast, and headed for school. The day was brisk, and she was glad she had her coat on. The bus was late, but it came after a while. Susie got on. Twenty minutes later, she arrived at school.

Does this sound like a story to you? There is a beginning, a middle, and an end. Susie wakes up, does some things, and then goes to school, but something is missing. Now read the next example:

Susie woke up Tuesday morning. She yawned, stretched, and made her way to the bathroom. She stared at her face in the mirror and realized that something had changed since the night before. She turned on the shower and waved her hand through the water. The shock of cold against her skin made her jump back. She held her wet hand against her chest and watched the spray of water. A strange fear grew around her heart like the tentacles of creeping ivy that ever so slowly envelopes an entire wall or side of a building. She turned off the water and dressed quickly. She ate a bowl of oatmeal for breakfast and headed for school. The day was brisk, and she was glad she had her coat on. She buried her face in the warm fleece. The faint scent of lilacs was still there. Mother's perfume. The bus was late, but it came after a while. Susie got on. Twenty minutes later, she arrived at school. The other children filed off one by one. Susie stayed in her seat and wept.

Which of the two above examples is a story? If you said the second one, you were right. Why? The first paragraph describes Susie's actions. You could spend pages doing that, but nothing *interesting* ever happens. In a story, there must be more than just action. There must also be ***conflict***.

In the second paragraph we see the conflict right away. Susie has somehow changed since the night before. She is fearful. She misses her mother enough to cry. We don't know all the details yet, but it is clear that whatever happened to her mother has affected Susie deeply and she will most likely struggle with this throughout the rest of the story.

In addition to action, all stories contain two essential elements: *Conflict* and *Resolution*. Conflict is the problem, and resolution is how the problem is resolved. Every story you read, every movie you watch is built on these two elements. Take away one or the other and you have no story, just a list of boring things that isn't worth reading or watching. Let's take a closer look at conflict and resolution now.

CONFLICT

As I mentioned in the previous section, the conflict in a story is the problem the protagonist faces during the course of the plot. The dictionary defines conflict as a clash of opposing ideas. In a story, the protagonist clashes with an opposing force of some kind. Maybe it is a villain out to destroy the world. Or it could be the challenge of climbing Mount Everest and surviving. Or it might be a struggle with his own emotional scars from some event in his past. Whatever the conflict is, that is where the heart of the story lies.

Objectives & Obstacles

To begin with, the protagonist must have a goal or objective. What is his primary motivation in this story? Does he want a certain girl to fall in love with him? Does he want revenge?

Does he want to win a battle? Catch the biggest fish in the ocean? Rescue a fellow soldier from a prisoner of war camp?

In your story you should ask yourself this question: What does my protagonist want more than anything else? Once you have that answer, then you should determine what or who is keeping him from reaching his goal. Spiderman wants to protect New York, but the Green Goblin is hell bent on destroying it—and him. Harry Potter wants to become a successful wizard, but Voldemort wants him dead. Anne Shirley wants a family, but her caregiver, Marilla Cuthbert, wants a boy instead of a girl.

Conflict comes in different varieties. There is man vs. man (often hero vs. villain), man vs. nature (hero vs. the sea, a mountain, an animal, etc.), and man vs. himself (hero vs. his own disability or circumstances.) Sometimes there is a romantic conflict, which is a form of man vs. man (or in this case man vs. woman.) Knowing what your protagonist wants and what is stopping him from getting it will determine which of these varieties the conflict will be.

Conflict is also organized into two other types of categories: internal and external. When the hero struggles with his own emotions, memories, or past, the conflict is internal. When the hero is at odds with something or someone outside himself, the conflict is external.

Internal Conflict

Let's return to our protagonist Susie. We left her sitting on the school bus crying. Why is she crying? Perhaps the night before, she witnessed her mother in a car accident. The car spun out of control and slipped into a swirling river. Mother survived and is in the hospital, but now Susie is filled with fear. Her fear stops her from interacting with the other children at school the way she normally would. During the course of the story she must overcome her fear and regain her confidence.

This conflict is internal. Susie wants to play with the kids at school. She wants to believe her mother will be well again. What is stopping her is the fear in her own mind.

External Conflict

Consider what would happen to our protagonist, Susie if she had not witnessed a car accident, but her mother's abduction? And now the kidnapper is out to get her? She cries on the bus because she does not know where to hide. So she must devise some way to protect herself and to rescue her mother at the same time. This is an external conflict. Susie wants her mother back, but the kidnapper is the obstacle preventing her from reaching her goal.

In *Gathering Blue,* Kira's mother dies leaving her alone, a crippled orphan. She wants to rebuild her cott (home), which was burned to cleanse it from her mother's sickness. The following excerpt reveals Kira's objective—to survive in a society where children like her are not usually allowed to live—and sets up the conflict between Kira and the other women of the village.

> "I heared them talking. They don't want you should stay. They be planning to turn you out, now that your mum be dead..."
>
> Kira felt her stomach tighten with fear. But she tried to keep her voice calm... "Who's 'they'?" she asked in an annoyed, superior tone.
>
> "Them women," [Matt] replied. "I heard them talking at the well...They want where your cott was..."
>
> Kira stared at him. It was terrifying, almost unbelievable, the casualness of the cruelty. In order to pen their disobedient toddlers and chickens, the women would turn her out of the village to be devoured by the beasts that waited in the woods to forage the Field." (10-11)

RESOLUTION

[Spoiler Warning: This section reveals the ending to the following stories: The Giver, Anne of Green Gables, "The Lady and the Tiger," & Tiger Rising.]

All good stories must come to an end, and in fiction every conflict must be resolved. There are only two possible outcomes for any conflict: success or failure. Success is when the protagonist gets what he wants. Failure is when the protagonist does not get what he wants.

Peter Parker wants to save New York from the evil Green Goblin. By the end of the movie, he succeeds by killing the villain. Anne Shirley wants to be allowed to live at Green Gables. She succeeds when the Cuthberts decide to let her live there and to adopt her as their own.

The resolution of your story should parallel the conflict. If the conflict is man vs. man, the good guy ends up defeating the bad guy. If it is man vs. nature, the hero succeeds at climbing Everest. If it is man vs. himself, the hero beats the odds against him and wins the race.

Failure may also occur, though today it is far less common for a hero in a movie or book to fail than to succeed. Audiences don't like their hero to fail. It's depressing. So failure is usually balanced by some small victory, even if it isn't exactly what we had in mind.

For example, in *The Tiger Rising*, the main characters Rob and Sistine want to free the tiger from its cage. When they make the attempt, however, Rob's father shoots and kills the tiger. It is a tragic end, but the fact that Rob's father was trying to protect his son opens the door for their damaged relationship to heal. It is a win/lose situation and the reader feels satisfied that something good came out of it after all.

There are times, however, when the author leaves it up to the reader to decide if the protagonist succeeds or fails. In the short story by Frank R. Stockton, "The Lady or the Tiger," the hero of the story stands before two doors. Behind one door is a tiger that will, should the door be opened, attack and kill the hero. Behind the other door is a beautiful lady to whom he will be instantly wed. The story ends as the hero reaches to open the door on the right, leaving the reader wondering whether he chose the lady or the tiger.

In Lois Lowry's Newbery Award winning novel *The Giver*, the protagonist, Jonas, escapes from his community. We are never told whether or not he reaches safety. The author leaves the ending up to reader's imagination

THE REST OF THE STORY

You have the beginning of the story (the conflict), and you have the end (the resolution.) What about the middle?

Draw a line on a blank piece of paper. At the left end of the line describe in a single sentence your protagonist's goal. (i.e. Susie wants her mother back.) Underneath it describe the conflict, the obstacle that is in her way. (i.e. Susie must rescue her mother from kidnappers.) On the right end of the line describe your resolution. How will your story end? Will he get the girl? Will he win the battle?

Now place a dot on the center of the line. Add another dot between the first dot and the left end of the line. Add another dot between the first dot and the right end of your line. It should look something like this:

——————·———·———·———

The dots represent what filmmakers call ***plot points***. They are the moments in the movie, or story, when something significant happens to move the story along. Movies usually have three main plot points. Books can have as many as the writer wishes, but for our purposes we will focus on three.

The first plot point is near the beginning of the story. It is where the conflict is first introduced. Susie receives a ransom note from her mother's kidnappers telling her she has 24 hours to deliver a ransom or mother dies.

Plot point #2 comes near the middle of the story. Just when the hero thinks things are going well, a really big problem arises, one that appears hopeless. Susie has discovered the kidnappers hideout and has snuck into the room to release her mom. All of a sudden the kidnapper appears behind her and knocks her unconscious.

The final plot point, or *climax*, is the final confrontation between the protagonist and whatever or whoever is opposing him. Susie wakes up to find herself tied up beside her mother. But she manages to break a mirror and cut her ropes with the broken glass. The kidnapper comes in before Susie can escape and there is a fight between them.

In a story where the resolution is success, Susie wins the fight and rescues her mom. The kidnapper is killed, injured or arrested. Justice is served. In a story where the resolution is failure, Susie will sacrifice herself in order to free her mother. She might throw herself in front of the villain's gun as her mother scrambles to safety, or Susie's mother might sacrifice herself for Susie. These are just examples, of course. And there is obviously more to Susie's story than just the plot points. Think of these points as the skeleton of your story. All the things that happen in between are your story's flesh and blood.

SUMMARY

All stories have action and conflict, and in fiction the conflict must be resolved. Sometimes the resolution is success, sometimes failure. The middle of a story has plot points, events within the story that move the plot along toward the final resolution.

Complete the following PLOT OUTLINE for your story.

PLOT OUTLINE

What is the protagonist's objective?

_____

_____

Who or what is standing in the way of him getting what he wants?

_____

_____

Is his conflict internal or external?

_____

_____

Which type of conflict is it?

       Man vs. man _____   Romantic _____

       Man vs. nature _____   Man vs. himself _____

How will this conflict be resolved?

_____

_____

_____

_____

_____

_____

_____

_____

_____

_____

_____

_____

Describe three plot points in your story:

Plot Point #1:

_____

_____

_____

_____

_____

_____

_____

Plot Point #2:

_____

_____

_____

_____

_____

_____

_____

Plot Point #3:

_____

_____

_____

_____

_____

_____

_____

LESSON #4
PERSPECTIVE

S o far we have discussed three important elements found in all stories. Characterization is the ingredients that make up each character: his physical appearance, personality traits, psychological traits, and background. The setting is the where and when of a story. The plot includes the beginning, middle and end of a story as well as everything that happens in between. By now you should have a fairly accurate picture of how your story will progress. You should know what your protagonist wants (the objective), what is standing in his way of getting it (the obstacle), and how he will overcome that obstacle (the resolution.)

Now we will answer another important question: **Who will tell your story?**

WHAT IS PERSPECTIVE?

In fiction, *perspective* is how a situation is seen and experienced through the eyes of the *narrator*, the narrator being the person who is telling the story. The narrator may be any one of the characters in a story or an omniscient being outside the story. Events that occur during the plot are told through that person's *point of view*.

Imagine you are at a baseball game. You are sitting in the bleachers just behind home plate. The pitcher throws the ball. The batter does not swing as it speeds past him into the catcher's mitt. The umpire shouts "Strike!" From where you are sitting you could see the direct path of the ball from the pitcher's hand to the mitt and you agree with the umpire.

Now imagine if you were sitting in some other part of the stadium. Above right field, for instance. Your perspective from this spot is much different than when you were sitting close to home plate. The very same pitch may look different to you now and when the umpire calls the strike, you might disagree. From your point of view the throw seems wide and should have been called a "ball."

All events experienced by more than one person, whether in fiction or in real life, can be retold from various perspectives. Each one will be a little different. The question is who is the right character to tell *your* story?

POINT OF VIEW

Before we answer that question, we need to first explore the three points of view that are used in storytelling. Each has drawbacks and benefits. Which one is right for your story will depend on which viewpoint you prefer and with which you feel most comfortable. At the end of this lesson you will have the opportunity to try them all.

First Person

In first person, the narrator speaks directly to the reader. He refers to himself as "I." Example: "I sat down at the table and stared at the bowl of oatmeal. I started to gag even before I put the first spoonful in my mouth."

One benefit of using first person is that you can reveal the narrator's thoughts and emotions easily. He can tell the reader what he is thinking and feeling. Also, the story seems immediate. As things happen to the narrator they happen to the reader, too. The drawback is that while you have great freedom to reveal the inner workings of your narrator, you are very limited in revealing the thoughts and emotions of all the other characters. Everyone and everything can be described only as your narrator sees them.

For example, if your narrator, John, were walking down the street and saw an older man in a trench coat walking toward him, you could not tell the reader what the man in the trench coat was thinking. You could only describe the scene through John's perspective.

In reading the following passage, we know that John feels uncomfortable in the man's presence, but we have no clue who the man is or what is going through his mind. This might be just what the author wants. If so, then first person is a good choice.

> The man in the trench coat approached me with slow, unsteady footsteps. His shoes dragged along the pavement as though they were weighted with lead. The man buried his face in the coat's collar. As we neared each other, the man stopped and lifted his face, his eyes tracking me as I passed, and a cold, nervous shiver ran up my spine.

Third Person

A story told from the third person point of view is more versatile than one told in first person. The narrator is not any character mentioned in the story. He is like God, looking down on this particular group of individuals describing their actions to the reader. The narrator uses "he," "she," and "they."

> John sat down at the breakfast table and stared at the bowl of oatmeal. He started to gag even before he put the first spoonful into his mouth.

With third person, the narrator might know everything about everyone (*omniscient*), or he might know a little about only one person (*limited*). He might be able to reveal the background and thoughts of many characters or he might only be able to tell us what he sees, as if he were just a bystander and knew as much about what is going on as we would if were standing there, too.

Here is where the point of view becomes important. In a first person story, the story is always told from the point of view of the narrator, who is usually one of the characters in the story. In a third person story, the point of view is a bit trickier than that. Let's take a look at four examples of third person narrative. The scene is the same in all of them, but the point of view is different in each one.

Example #1:

The man in the trench coat approached John with slow, unsteady footsteps. His shoes dragged along the pavement as though they were weighted with lead. The man buried his face in his coat collar. As they neared each other, the man stopped and lifted his face, his eyes tracking John as he passed, and a cold, nervous shiver ran up John's spine.

Example # 2:

Oscar approached the boy with slow, unsteady footsteps. His shoes dragged along the pavement and he buried his face in the coat's collar. Since the accident, his feet had felt like lead and their heaviness reminded him of the way Frankenstein's monster walked in the movies. As he and the boy neared each other, Oscar stopped and lifted his face. He had intended to smile, but then changed his mind when he saw the frightened expression on the boy's face.

Example #3:

Oscar approached John with slow, unsteady footsteps. His shoes dragged along the pavement and he buried his face in the collar of his trench coat. Since the accident, his

Continued...

Example #3, continued:

Oscar approached John with slow, unsteady footsteps. His shoes dragged along the pavement and he buried his face in the collar of his trench coat. Since the accident, his feet had felt like lead and their heaviness reminded him of the way Frankenstein's monster walked in the movies. As they neared each other, Oscar stopped and lifted his face, his eyes tracking John as he passed. John averted his gaze. He hurried his pace, eager to reach the intersection and the safety of heavy traffic. Despite his better judgment, he stole a glance over his shoulder. The man in the trench coat was still there, watching him. A cold, nervous shiver ran up John's spine.

Example #4:

Oscar approached John with slow, unsteady footsteps. His shoes dragged along the pavement as though they were lead. He buried his face in the collar of his trench coat. As they neared each other, Oscar stopped and lifted his face, his eyes tracking John as he passed. John averted his gaze. He hurried his pace and stole a glance over his shoulder. The man in the trench coat was still there, watching him.

In example #1 the story is told from John's point of view. We see what he sees, feel what he feels. In the second example, the point of view is reversed. This time we observe events through Oscar's perspective. Both Oscar and John's perspectives are described in example #3. In the fourth example, the story is told in a limited point of view. The narrator does not reveal the thoughts and emotions of either character, only an objective observation of what is happening between them.

Second Person

Second person is rarely used in fiction. The narrator addresses the reader as though speaking directly to him. For example:

> You sit at the breakfast table and stare at the bowl of oatmeal. You gag before you even put the first spoonful into your mouth.

In this narration, the story is happening to the reader rather than to a character in the story. This does not work well unless the story requires the reader to be directly involved (such as in choose-your-own-adventure books.) Sometimes a narrator might use second person in the beginning or the end of a story to introduce him to the plot and characters. But the rest of the story will usually be in first or third person.

TENSE

In addition to deciding *who* will tell your story, it is also important to know *when* the story will be told. The tense has nothing to do with what century or time of day your story takes place, but whether the story takes place in the past, present or future. To make things simple, we will rule out future. Like second person narration, future tense is not used often in fiction except in limited circumstances. The vast majority of stories are written in either past or present tense.

Past Tense

Past tense means that the story is told as if it has already occurred. The narrator tells the reader about something that happened yesterday, last week, last year, etc. Therefore the verbs will be past tense: jumped, ran, slept, ate, etc. For example:

> I sat down at the table and stared at the bowl of oatmeal. I started to gag even before I put the first spoonful in my mouth.

There are definite benefits to writing in past tense and it is the most common tense used in fiction today. Since the story has already taken place, the narrator has a vast amount of knowledge of events and can give the reader clues to what will happen later. This is called *foreshadowing*.

> The man in the trench coat approached John with slow, unsteady footsteps. His shoes dragged along the pavement as though they were weighted with lead. As they neared each other, the man stopped and lifted his face, his eyes tracking John as he passed, and a cold, nervous shiver ran up John's spine. Little did he know that this stranger would someday save his life.

The drawbacks to using past tense are few. However, sometimes an author wants the story to feel more immediate, as if it is happening right now. Then he will use present tense.

Present Tense

Present tense means that the story is happening *now*. The narrator describes events as if they were occurring at that very moment. The verbs are present tense: jump, run, sleep, eat, etc. For example:

> I sit down at the table and stare at the bowl of oatmeal. I start to gag even before I put the first spoonful in my mouth.

The benefits to using present tense is that the pace of the story is fast and the reader feels as though he is standing right beside the narrator as events unfold. He is not being told the story; he is experiencing it right along with the narrator.

> The man in the trench coat approaches John with slow, unsteady footsteps. His shoes drag along the pavement as though they are weighted with lead. As they near each other, the man stops and lifts his face, his eyes tracking John as he passes, and a cold, nervous shiver runs up John's spine.

The drawbacks to using present tense are that the narrator cannot foreshadow future events, and sometimes the story might be too close to the reader for comfort. Whether you choose first or third person point of view, and past or present tense is a matter of taste more than anything. Play with different perspectives while writing the early draft of your story.

SUMMARY

Perspective is the point of view from which a story is told. In fiction, the point of view is most often first or third person. In first person, the narrator refers to himself as "I." In third person, the narrator refers to all the characters in the story as "they" or "them." Stories can be told in the past or present tense.

Complete the following PERSPECTIVE WORKSHEET using a scene from your own story.

PERSPECTIVE WORKSHEET

Write the opening paragraph from your own story from several different perspectives. Then choose which point of view and tense you will use to write your story.

First Person, Past Tense:

_____

_____

_____

_____

_____

_____

_____

_____

_____

_____

_____

Third Person Past Tense:

_____

_____

_____

_____

_____

_____

_____

_____

_____

_____

_____

First Person, Present Tense:

_____

_____

_____

_____

_____

_____

_____

_____

_____

_____

_____

_____

Third Person, Present Tense:

_____

_____

_____

_____

_____

_____

_____

_____

_____

_____

_____

_____

Which perspective do you prefer for your story?

_____

_____

LESSON #5
IMAGERY

Imagine you have just come inside after a rainstorm. Your younger brother or sister, who has been in the house all day, asks you what the weather is like. You might respond by simply saying, "It's raining." But what if the person asking the question was a visitor from outer space and had never seen rain before. How would you describe it then?

Imagery is a mental picture. In literature, the words we read on the page help us form these mental pictures. How the author chooses to describe something, such as a rainstorm, will determine what kind of picture it will be.

ALL FIVE SENSES

Close your eyes and think back to the last time you stood outside in the rain. Was it a heavy storm, or a light sprinkle? How did the droplets feel against your skin? Were you cold? Did you shiver? What did the air smell like? If you were in the mountains, could you smell the scent of pine trees in the air? If you were near the ocean, did you smell the sea? Describe the experience on the worksheet at the end of this lesson. Include as much detail as possible.

Read over your description. How many of your five senses did you include? Would someone from a dry climate be able to imagine himself standing in the rain just from reading your words?

Imagery involves all five senses: sight, sound, touch, taste and smell. For example, if you were to describe the inside of a movie theater, you might include the smell of buttered popcorn or the way the soles of your shoes stick to the floor when you walk. When describing the beach, you might describe the texture of wet sand between your toes, the taste of salt on your lips, or the sound of the waves crashing on the shore.

Imagery is used in every aspect of storytelling, including setting, action, and characterization. Below are two examples of imagery from Kate DiCamillo's *The Tiger Rising*. These brief but vivid descriptions help us form clear pictures of the characters they describe.

<u>Sense of Smell</u>
"[Billy] followed Rob and sat down right next to him. He pushed his face so close that Rob could smell his breath. It was bad breath. It smelled metallic and rotten."

FIGURATIVE LANGUAGE

Writers often use words in creative ways to make a story, or even a specific moment in a story, come alive. While describing something is good, using figurative language to help the reader imagine what is being described is often better. There are seven forms of figurative speech, each effective in creating imagery in its own way.

Metaphors & Similes

Comparing one object to another is another effective tool of imagery. A metaphor compares two objects by saying one object *is* the other object. *The full moon is a shiny new quarter.* A simile compares two objects using the words *like* or *as*. *The full moon is like a shiny new quarter,* or *the full moon is as shiny as a new quarter.*

In his Newbery Award winning novel *Maniac Magee,* author Jerry Spinelli uses imagery to add dimension to what might otherwise be lackluster descriptions:

"The book came flapping like a wounded duck and fell at Jeffrey's feet." (13)

> "The peeling paint came off like cornflakes." (131)

> "He and Amanda and the suitcase were like a rock in a stream; the school-goers just flowed to the left and right around them." (11)

The similes above draw concrete pictures in the mind. The comparisons are bold and imaginative. A book flying at someone like a wounded duck creates a much bolder image than just a book falling down at his feet.

Metaphors achieve the same effect, except through more subtle means. The following examples are also from *Maniac Magee:*

> "He's paralyzed, a mouse in front of the yawning maw of a python." (18)

> "As whistles go, Mrs. Pickwell's was one of the all-time greats. It reeled in every Pickwell kid for dinner every night." (20)

In the first metaphor, a young boy paralyzed with fear is compared to a mouse about to be eaten by a hungry snake. He is not *like* a mouse. He *is* a mouse.

The second example is even subtler than the first. The two objects being compared are a mother's whistle and a fishing rod. Though, no mention is made of the rod, the verb is our clue. The whistle "reeled" in children for dinner – just like a rod reels in fish. The images created by both of these examples are much more interesting than just saying a boy was scared or kids came home for dinner when their mother called.

Personification

To take comparison to still a subtler level, authors often infuse inanimate objects with human characteristics, a technique called *personification*. Let's look once more at Jerry Spinelli's *Maniac Magee:*

> "Within an hour or two, the holiday would come bounding down the stairs and squealing 'round the tinseled trees of Two Mills." (112)

> "For most of November, winter toyed with Two Mills, whispered in its ear, tickled it under the chin." (106)

> "January slipped an icy finger under his collar and down his back." (125)

Do holidays bound down staircases? Does winter whisper in people's ears? Do months of the year have fingers? Of course not, but by imbuing them with human-like traits, the author has created vivid images in our minds of things that might otherwise have seemed dull.

Alliteration & Onomatopoeia

Two additional forms of figurative language focus more on the sounds of words as opposed to their meaning. Alliteration is when two or more words in close proximity to each other use the same sound or letter repeatedly. This is often used in poetry, but can also be effective in narrative writing.

The silly snake slid into its hole.

Here, the alliteration appears in the repetition of the letter 's' at the beginning of silly, snake, and slid.

Stuart was lost in the forest.

Here, the alliteration appears in the repetition of the sound 'st' in Stuart, lost, and forest. However, alliteration can be used with any repeated letter or sound, with two words or more.

Onomatopoeia also uses sound to emphasize words, but in a different way. Rather than describing the way something sounds, these words try to recreate sound. Here are some examples:

Whoosh! Zap! Bam! Clickety-clack Ka-boom! Swish

The list of onomatopoeia words is extensive, and you can even make up your own. What does a marble sound like when it drops into a puddle of water? What does the wind blowing through a tree sound like, or the cry of a newborn kitten?

"Jaberwocky", a famous 19th century poem, which appeared in the novel Through the Looking Glass by Lewis Carroll, is an excellent example of both alliteration and onomatopoeia. Read it out loud and note the way Carroll uses sound to express meaning and create a sense of rhythm. These forms of speech can be used just as effectively in storytelling, though likely not to this extent.

JABBERWOCKY
By Lewis Carroll

'Twas brillig, and the slithy toves
   Did gyre and gimble in the wabe:
All mimsy were the borogoves,
   And the mome raths outgrabe.

"Beware the Jabberwock, my son!
   The jaws that bite, the claws that catch!
Beware the Jubjub bird, and shun
   The frumious Bandersnatch!"

He took his vorpal sword in hand;
   Long time the manxome foe he sought—
So rested he by the Tumtum tree
   And stood awhile in thought.

And, as in uffish thought he stood,
   The Jabberwock, with eyes of flame,

Came whiffling through the tulgey wood,
And burbled as it came!

One, two! One, two! And through and through
The vorpal blade went snicker-snack!
He left it dead, and with its head
He went galumphing back.

"And hast thou slain the Jabberwock?
Come to my arms, my beamish boy!
O frabjous day! Callooh! Callay!"
He chortled in his joy.

'Twas brillig, and the slithy toves
Did gyre and gimble in the wabe:
All mimsy were the borogoves,
And the mome raths outgrabe.

Hyperbole

Hyperbole is an exaggerated way of describing things in order to get a point across. For example, you might say the day is so hot out you could fry eggs on the sidewalk, or that a man is so thin you could see right through him, or I'm so hungry I could eat a horse. These are exaggerations, of course. You can't really see through a skinny person or cook food on a hot sidewalk, but the hyperbole emphasizes what the speaker, or writer, is trying to say. Here is an example of hyperbole from the American folk legend, Paul Bunyon.

"Well now, one winter it was so cold that all the geese flew backward and all the fish moved south and even the snow turned blue. Late at night, it got so frigid that all spoken words froze solid afore they could be heard. People had to wait until sunup to find out what folks were talking about the night before."

Idioms

Idioms are words or sets of words that have more than one meaning. In other words, what the words say and what they mean are two different things. Here are some examples:

A piece of cake (very easy)

Out of the blue (with no warning)

Fish out of water (being somewhere you don't belong)

Birdbrain (someone who is not very smart)

Hold your horses (wait)

Play it by ear (improvise)

SYMBOLISM

The final tool of imagery is *symbolism*, using an object or image to represent a theme or to foreshadow a future event in the story. Symbolism is particularly common in poetry, but it is popular in filmmaking and storytelling as well. In the book *Surviving the Applewhites* by Stephanie S. Tolan, the metamorphosis of caterpillars into butterflies parallels the changes the protagonist, Jake, experiences throughout the course of the story.

Color plays an important role in Lois Lowry's book *Gathering Blue*. Blue, we are told, is "the color of the sky, of peace,"[1] and finding it suggests Kira's ability to bring peace back to her people.

Rob, in *The Tiger Rising*, struggles with painful memories of his dead mother. Rather than face them, he keeps them buried deep inside, like locking them inside a suitcase. His feelings "are straining to come out," foreshadowing a time when he will have to face them head-on.

> "Rob had a way of not-thinking about things. He imagined himself as a suitcase that was too full, like the one that he had packed when they left Jacksonville after the funeral. He made all his feelings go inside the suitcase; he stuffed them in tight and then sat on the suitcase and locked it shut. That was the way he not-thought about things. Sometimes it was hard to keep the suitcase shut. But now he had something to put on top of it. The tiger." (187)

Symbols, such as butterflies, a particular color, or a suitcase help the reader to connect with the story by comparing the overall theme of the story to something the reader will understand.

---

[1] *Gathering Blue*, Lois Lowry, p. 187

SUMMARY

Imagery is the mental pictures we form in our minds when reading a story. Imagery utilizes all five senses in descriptions. Figurative language and symbolism are also useful techniques in helping the reader visualize the setting and other aspects of the story.

Complete the following IMAGERY WORKSHEET to help make your descriptions more complex and vivid.

IMAGERY WORKSHEET

Using the five senses and comparisons, describe the following setting. The final location should be a setting from your own story:

RAIN STORM:

Sight:

_____

_____

Sound:

_____

_____

Smell:

_____

_____

Touch:

_____

_____

Taste:

_____

_____

Metaphor/Simile:

_____

_____

Personification:

_____

_____

Other:

_____

_____

A BAKERY:

Sight:

_____

_____

Sound:

_____

_____

Smell:

_____

_____

Touch:

_____

_____

Taste:

_____

_____

Metaphor/Simile:

_____

_____

Personification:

_____

_____

Other:

_____

_____

A SCENE FROM YOUR OWN STORY:

Sight:

_____

_____

Sound:

_____

_____

Smell:

_____

_____

Touch:

_____

_____

Taste:

_____

_____

Metaphor/Simile:

_____

_____

Personification:

_____

_____

Other:

_____

_____

Select an Object to symbolize the theme of your story. It should be something simple like the butterfly, the tree, or the suitcase mentioned in the lesson.

The Theme:

_____

_____

The Symbol:

_____

_____

Write paragraph of description using one or more examples
of imagery from your worksheet.

_____

_____

_____

_____

_____

_____

_____

_____

_____

_____

_____

_____

_____

_____

_____

_____

LESSON #6
DIALOGUE

Dialogue is conversation. In fiction, it is the spoken words written on a page. In real life, people talk to one another. One person says one thing. Another responds, and so forth. Characters in books talk to each other, too. This lesson will focus on three aspects of written dialogue: purpose, format, and tag lines.

PURPOSE

Why do you need dialogue? Why not just tell the story from beginning to end without interruption? There are several reasons for dialogue. Dialogue reveals information about the characters, helps the plot progress, and creates a sense of realism for the readers.

Characterization
In O. Henry's short story, "The Last Leaf," we discover that the character, Behrman, is from Germany by the accent written into his dialogue. We also know he is a bit impatient

67

and judgmental by what he says and how he says it. However, we also know that he has a sympathetic heart.

> "Vass!" he cried. "Is dere people in de world mit der foolishness to die because leafs dey drop off from a confounded vine? I haf not heard of such a thing. No, I will not bose as a model for your fool hermit-dunderhead. Vy do you allow dot silly pusiness to come in der brain of her? Ach, dot poor leetle Miss Yohnsy."

As in "The Last Leaf," using dialect (accented language) in dialogue can reveal what area of the country or world a character was raised. It can also reveal age and level of education. In *Gathering Blue,* Matt is a young boy from an impoverished section of his community. Note the contrast between Matt's childlike use of language and the more mature language of his older friend, Kira:

> "I been on a horrid long journey," Matt told her proudly.
> She sniffed and smiled. "And you never washed, not once, while you were gone."
> "There be no time for washing," he scoffed. "I brung you a giftie," he told her eagerly, his eyes dancing with excitement.
> "What is it that you held up at the Gathering? I couldn't see it."
> "I brung you two things. A big and a little. The big be coming still. But I gots the little here in my pockie." (186)

Plot Progression

Dialogue can further the plot of a story. This means that the events in the story are described through the conversation between two or more characters. The following dialogue from "The Open Boat" by Stephen Crane occurs between two characters stranded on a life boat in the middle of the ocean:

"Look! There's a man on the shore!"
"Where?"
"There! See 'im? See 'im?"
"Yes, sure! He's walking along."
"Now he's stopped. Look! He's facing us!"
"He's waving at us!"
"So he is! By thunder!"
"Ah, now, we're all right! Now we're all right! There'll be a boat out here for us in half an hour."
"He's going on. He's running. He's going up to that house there."

The author could have just told us that a man on the beach saw the boat and went running. Instead he revealed this plot point through conversation. We sense the excitement and hope in the men's words, emotion that would have been lost to us had that moment been simply narrated.

Creating a Sense of Realism

Finally, dialogue gives the story and characters a realism that just cannot be achieved through straight narration. Compare the narrated story "The Lady, or The Tiger" with stories with dialogue, such as "The Open Boat" and "The Last Leaf."

Which of these stories seem more up close and personal to you?

In *The Tiger Rising*, Rob and Sistine go to an older, African-American housekeeper, Willie May, to ask her opinion about what they should do about the tiger in the woods. Instead of describing the encounter through narration, the author brings us right into the conversation with dialogue:

> "Willie May sat down on the bed. A cloud of dust rose up around her. "Lord God," she said. "What you two children got in a cage?"
>
> "It's a tiger," Rob said. He felt like he had to be the one who said it. He was the one who found the tiger. He was the one who had the keys to the cage.
>
> "A what?" said Willie May.
>
> "A tiger," said Sistine.
>
> "Do Jesus!" exclaimed Willie May.
>
> "It's true," said Sistine.
>
> Willie May shook her head. She looked up at the ceiling. She let out her breath in a loud slow hiss of disapproval. "All right," she said. "Why don't you all show me where you got this tiger locked up in a cage?"" (93)

Though it may seem easier to simply narrate a story, including some dialogue will involve the reader in a much more personal way. Narrative without dialogue is nothing more than a summary. However, remember that dialogue must serve a purpose. In real life, most conversation is dull and pointless. We talk about the weather and the price of gasoline. Most of what is said between two people has no real purpose except to pass the time. In fiction, dialogue should sound realistic without being frivolous. Make sure every conversation in your story satisfies one of the purposes mentioned above.

FORMAT

Dialogue looks different than narrative text. In narrative text, the words are written in paragraph form. The first line is indented five spaces from the left margin. For the most part, complete sentences are used, as are normal forms of punctuation. Narrative text includes description, action, background, and any other information that is not spoken by a character. The rules are generally the same with dialogue, with a few exceptions.

Punctuation

When characters speak, their words are placed between quotation marks. For example, if Jane were to tell John that the sun is setting, it would look like this:

"John, the sun is setting."

Notice that the period is located *inside* the quotation mark. This would also apply if a comma were required:

"John, the sun is setting," said Jane.

If the sentence ends in a question mark or exclamation mark, it must also go inside the quotation mark.

> "John, the sun is setting!" said Jane.

Spacing

In narrative text, the first line of any new paragraph is indented. The same holds true for dialogue. When a person begins to speak, begin the line of dialogue as if it were a new paragraph. Indent five spaces from the left margin. If the character's dialogue contains more than one sentence, just continue writing them like a regular paragraph. Just remember to end the entire comment with the quotation mark.

> "John, the sun is setting. I am feeling rather tired. Would you mind if I went to bed a little earlier than usual?"

If two people are having a conversation, a new paragraph is needed each time the speaker changes.

> "John, the sun is setting," said Jane. "I am tired. Would you mind if I went to bed a little earlier than usual?"
> "Not at all," John replied.
> "Thank you. I will see you in the morning."

Structure

Dialogue does not always follow the rules of correct grammar. Dialogue in fiction should sound like real life conversations. The above examples might be appropriate for a story about two adults. It would not work in a story about teenagers in high school where the following example may be more suitable.

> "Hey."
>
> "Hey," replied Jake as he slid a stick of gum into his mouth.
>
> "Seen Billy?"
>
> "Nah. You?"
>
> "Uh-uh." Tom patted his back pocket and found it empty. "Got anymore of that gum?" he asked.

TAG LINES

I will just say a few words about tag lines. A tag line tells who is speaking a line of dialogue.

> "John, the sun is setting," said Jane.

Said Jane is the tag line. Tag lines come in many forms: she cried, he exclaimed, she asked, he whispered, an on and on and on. There are only two rules to remember when it comes to tag lines:

Rule #1: Use a tag line to clarify who is speaking.

Rule #2: Do not over use them.

Look at the earlier example of dialogue from "The Open Boat." Notice that there are no tag lines. Reading this out of context may seem confusing. We don't know who is saying what. However, if you were reading this in the context of the story you would know that there are two characters speaking, the Oiler and the Correspondent. Since a new paragraph is required each time the speaker changes, it is fairly easy to see that the lines of dialogue jump back and forth from the oiler to the correspondent.

In the example from *The Tiger Rising*, however, there are three characters speaking. Therefore, some clarification is needed. Tag lines are inserted so that we know who is saying what. A good test to see if a tag line is needed in any particular dialogue is to read the section out loud to someone else and see if they know who is speaking. If it gets confusing at all, use a tag line. But don't get carried away with tag lines! It is far too easy to over use them, such as in the example below:

"John, the sun is setting," said Jane.
"Yes, it is," said John.
"Would you mind if I go to bed early?" asked Jane.
"Not at all," said John.

It gets annoying after a while. Think of tag lines like seasoning. A little salt goes a long way.

Finally, exercise caution in getting too creative with your tag lines. As tempting as it may be to use every synonym that exists for 'said,' it is best to stick with the tried and true. A little variation is okay, but not too much. To get a feel for how to use tag lines effectively, use a highlighter the next time you read a book. Highlight all the tag lines and list the words used for 'said.' Chances are it will be a short list.

SUMMARY

Dialogue is the written conversation within a story and serves several purposes: to reveal information about the character, to move the plot along, and to make the story more realistic. New lines of dialogue should always begin on a new line and should be placed between quotation marks. Tag lines clarify who is speaking and should be used sparingly.

Complete the following DIALOGUE ACTIVITY to help you become more comfortable with using dialogue in your own story.

DIALOGUE ACTIVITY

Imagine you have two characters in a story, William and Bobby. They are young boys walking by a candy shop. They stop and gaze in the window at the array of sweets. They decide to go inside to buy some, but neither of them have enough money to buy what they want. In the ensuing conversation, William and Bobby search their pockets for loose change and bargain with each other about whether or not they will combine their money and how they will share the candy once they buy it.

Write a brief dialogue between William and Bobby in the lines below. Keep in mind what you have learned about the format, purposes, and tag lines of dialogue.

_____

_____

_____

_____

_____

_____

_____

_____

_____

_____

_____

_____

_____

_____

_____

Now that you have completed the above exercise, choose two characters from your own story and write a scene of dialogue for them.

_____

_____

_____

_____

_____

_____

_____

_____

_____

_____

_____

_____

_____

_____

_____

_____

_____

_____

_____

_____

_____

_____

_____

_____

_____

_____

CONCLUSION: POLISHING YOUR STORY

·◆·

Throughout the course of this workbook you have learned the key elements to all stories: characterization, plot, perspective, setting, imagery and dialogue. Like the bricks used in building a house, these elements form the building blocks of your story. You should have completed six worksheets, one for each lesson. Using ideas gleaned from these exercises, you should also have constructed a rough draft of your story. However, don't take a vacation. Your story isn't finished yet.

FORMAT

At present, your story is either hand-written or typed. If it is hand-written, you should prepare a clean, typed copy of your story. The following format guidelines are preferred (see Diagram 1):

A.   Set margins at 1 inch.
B.   Double-space text.

C. Place title one third of the way down the first page.

D. Begin the text of your story half way down the first page, below the title.

E. Author's name may appear below title or in upper right hand corner.

F. Indent the first line of each paragraph.

G. Place page numbers at the bottom center of each page.

Title
Author Name

_____

_____

_____

_____

_____

_____

p. #

REVISION

The next step to writing a great story is to polish it. This is called the *revision* process. To make revising your story a little easier, follow the suggestions below:

1: Read your story out loud. Hearing your story will make it easier to spot spelling and grammar errors in the text and inconsistencies in the plot. Mark the changes that need to be made.

2: Choose two people to read and critique your story. Tell them to be honest. You do not want empty praise. You want honest criticism. Ask them to write down specific examples of what they liked and did not like in your story.

3: Spend more time editing than you did writing your story. It should take three, four or even more drafts before a story feels "just right." Don't be afraid to change things. Change will usually make it better.

4: Let it breathe. After you have re-read your story, had two people critique it, and spent a good deal of time revising it, put it away for a while. Slip it in a drawer or a box. Don't look at it for a few days or a few weeks. Then take it out and read it again. If it needs some more revising, then get back to work! If you're happy with it, then congratulations! Your story is finished.

ABOUT LANGUAGE

Do you own a thesaurus? If not, go out and buy one—right now! A thesaurus is similar to a dictionary in that you can look up words alphabetically. You are not looking for a word's definition, but a list of words that mean the same or almost the same thing. For example, if you were to look up the word *walk* in a thesaurus you would find a list of words such as *stroll, amble, march,* and *stride.* You can then use one of those words instead of *walk* when writing your story. Consider the following three sentences:

> Jamie walked to the party.
>
> Jamie pranced to the party.
>
> Jamie trudged to the party.

All three sentences mean the same thing. Or do they? While the words walk, prance, and trudge all mean to move from one place to another, they each convey a distinctly different sense of emotion. Walk is straightforward, with little or no emotion attached. Prance suggests happiness, excitement. Trudge suggests boredom or depression.

A common saying for writers is "show, don't tell." It is easy to tell the reader that someone is sad, or happy, or frightened. But showing them these emotions is far more interesting. How does Rob, from *The Tiger Rising,* feel in the following example?

> "[Rob] ran at his father and attacked him. He beat him with his fists. He kicked him. But his father stood like a wall. He held the gun up over his head and kept his eyes open and took each hit without blinking." (106)

The right words can tell a lot more about a character than just emotion. Jerry Spinelli could have told us that his character Maniac Magee was a fast runner, but instead he says:

> "They say if you knew he was coming and you sprinkled salt on the ground and he ran over it, within two or three blocks he would be as slow as everybody else." (1)

When revising your story, look for words and phrases that seem dull or unimaginative. Replace them with words that are more meaningful and creative. Remember to show, not tell.

PUBLISH

Once your story is complete, the final step is to publish it. This can be achieved in a number of ways. Print several copies and distribute them to friends and family members. If you are part of a writing class, include all your stories in an anthology and publish it on your class website or with a print-on-demand publisher, such as *www.lulu.com*. You may also submit your story to magazines that accept material from young writers. Child-friendly publishers are listed in *Writer's Market*, available through *Writer's Digest Book Club* or at your local book retailer.

Of course, there is always the option of writing just for the fun of it. Whether you publish your story or not, whether your story is perfect or not, give yourself a pat on the back because YOU DID IT! You are a writer!

Title

Written by _____

_____

_____

_____

_____

_____

_____

_____

_____

_____

_____

_____

_____

_____

_____

_____

_____

_____

_____

About the Author
LAURISA WHITE REYES

Laurisa White Reyes is the former Editor-in-Chief of *Middle Shelf Magazine*, the Senior Editor of Skyrocket Press, and an English professor at College of the Canyons in Santa Clarita, California. She is also the author of *Teaching Kids to Write Well: Six Secrets Every Grown-up Should Know,* as well as several novels, including the 2015 SCBWI Spark Award winner, *The Storytellers.*

Website: www.laurisawhitereyes.com
Blog: laurisareyes.blogspot.com

Teaching Kids
To Write ~~Good~~ *Well*

Six Secrets Every Grown-Up Should Know

Second Edition

Laurisa White Reyes

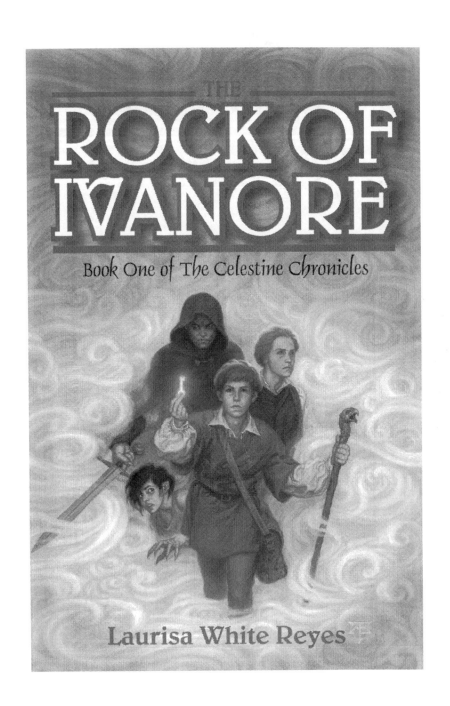

THE
ROCK OF
IVANORE

Book One of The Celestine Chronicles

Laurisa White Reyes

The LAST ENCHANTER

Book Two of The
Celestine Chronicles

Laurisa White Reyes

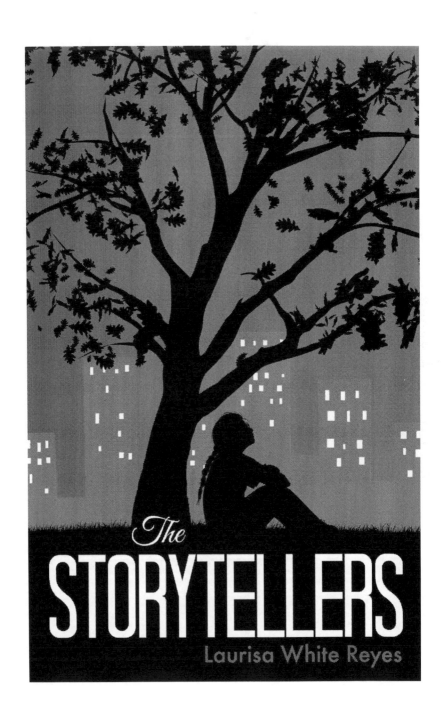

EVERNIGHT
TEEN

CONTACT

LAURISA WHITE REYES

LAURISA WHITE REYES

The CRYSTAL *Keeper*

BOOKS 1-3

WORKS CITED

Crane, Stephan. *The Open Boat and Other Stories*. Project Gutenberg. n.d. Web. 31 Aug 2015.

DiCamillo, Kate. *The Tiger Rising*. Cambridge, MA: Candlewick Press, Inc., 2001. Print.

Henry, O. "The Last Leaf." *Project Gutenberg*. n.d. Web. 31 Aug 2015.

Lowry, Lois. *Gathering Blue*. New York, NY: Houghton Mifflin Harcourt, 2000. Print.

Reyes, Laurisa White. *The Rock of Ivanore*. Terre Haute, IN: Tanglewood Press, 2012. Print.

Rodda, Emily. *Rowan of Rin*. Australia: Scholastic Australia, 1993. Print.

Skye, Obert. *Leven Thumps and the Gateway to Foo*. Salt Lake City, UT: Shadow Mountain, 2005. Print.

Spinelli, Jerry. *Maniac Magee*. New York, NY: Little, Brown & Co., 1990. Print.

Made in the USA
Middletown, DE
22 January 2018